Moments In Time

To Angus, Megan and Rowena

Moments In Time

Sketches Around Inverness

Illustrations by Merrill MacWilliam • Text by Rab MacWilliam

KESSOCK BOOKS

Merrill graduated from Glasgow School of Art in the mid-1970s. She has been a freelance illustrator ever since and continues to enjoy the challenge of being asked to draw and paint a variety of subjects.

With a lifelong interest in natural history, animals and birds are a favourite theme. She equally enjoys capturing a local landmark or landscape, as shown in this book.

Merrill lives in Inverness with her husband George. Visit www.merrillmacwilliam.com to view more.

Rab was born and brought up in Inverness, and he attended the Crown School and Royal Academy. He studied at the Universities of Edinburgh and Essex in the 1970s, and he has been employed in book and magazine publishing, in editorial and management roles, for forty years.

Today he works in a freelance capacity, and is a magazine and book packager and publisher, editor and writer. He has written twelve books on a variety of subjects.

Rab is married and lives in Stoke Newington, North London. Merrill is his sister-in-law.

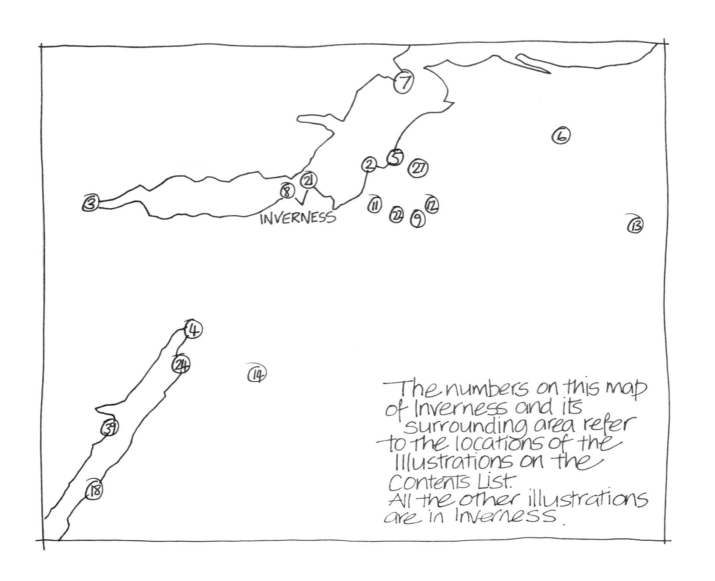

INVERNESS

The numbers on this map of Inverness and its surrounding area refer to the locations of the Illustrations on the Contents List.
All the other illustrations are in Inverness.

Illustrations

Illustrator Introduction: Merrill MacWilliam

I am fortunate to live in such a beautiful place. Inverness has been my home for a long time, and I have worked in the city as an illustrator and artist, a tutor of community art classes and a part-time college lecturer. Our three children grew up here, and now our grandchildren are also starting their lives in the Highlands.

Inverness has altered a great deal over the thirty years I have lived here. Some of the changes could be reflected upon with wistful regret but, on the whole, Inverness has become a vibrant place, a city with much to offer. Many of my drawings show buildings familiar to those who remember old Inverness, but I have also included subjects which celebrate the evolving Inverness of the twenty-first century as well as the splendid scenery of the wider area.

Over the years I have had the opportunity, as a freelance illustrator, to depict aspects of Inverness and its surroundings. In so doing, I have learned much about this area's fascinating history. When I was asked by Kessock Books to create a book of drawings of Inverness, it presented an ideal opportunity to work with Rab. Together with his knowledge of the area and his creative writing skills, I was confident that we could produce an informative and quirky book, and I hope you feel that we have succeeded in this aim.

Pen and ink and pencil are my favourite mediums for my work. I hope that the illustrations in the following pages convey the atmosphere, natural beauty and sense of history found in Inverness and its surrounding area.

I would like to thank Rab very much for his text, which I feel complements my drawings well. I would also like to thank Kessock Books for providing me with this opportunity, and many thanks to Speedprint for their help and expertise. Finally, I thank you, the reader, for picking up this book, and I hope you find it as interesting and enjoyable as Rab and I did when we were compiling it.

Merrill MacWilliam, Inverness, September 2015

Author Introduction: Rab MacWilliam

As you will no doubt gather from our surnames, Merrill and I are related. She is married to my brother George and has lived in Inverness for well over thirty years. I was born, brought up and educated in what was then the town of Inverness, and have lived in London for forty years.

I have managed to scrape a livelihood through editing, book and magazine publishing and writing, enterprises in which I seem to have a modest talent. Merrill, however, is a gifted artist in both drawing and oil painting, and she has worked for BBC Scotland, illustrated several books, staged a number of successful and highly praised exhibitions of her work, and much else besides.

When the opportunity arose for Merrill to provide for Kessock Books a number of drawings on the Inverness area, I was flattered that she asked me to write the accompanying text. We are both very familiar with, and fond of, Inverness and its surroundings and with the Highlands generally, and we readily agreed on the subjects which should be included.

My text is short, descriptive and designed to set a context for the main purpose of the book, which is to highlight Merrill's illustrative skills, visionary imagination and insightful perspectives on a part of the world which she loves. I only hope my words satisfactorily complement the originality of Merrill's works.

Rab MacWilliam, London, September 2015

1. **Across The River:** Panorama over the Ness

This panoramic view gazes westward across the River Ness from the top of Castle Hill. To the left is Ness Bank Church beside the river, with Inverness Cathedral, occupying the centre of Merrill's illustration, on the opposite bank. The river stretches for 12 miles, beginning at the northern tip of Loch Ness and running through Loch Dochfour, where the Caledonian Canal diverges from the river. The Ness then drifts past the Islands and flows through the heart of the city before entering the Beauly Firth. In medieval times it was the second-fastest-flowing river in Britain. The name 'Inverness' derives from the Gaelic 'Inbhir Nis' or 'mouth of the river'.

Ness Bank Church, built in 1901, is a Church of Scotland, red sandstone building in the Gothic revival style and is built on a slope leading down to the river. It was Category C listed in 1971. Inverness Cathedral, also known as the Church of Saint Andrew, is Scottish Episcopalian and is the seat of the Bishop of Moray, Ross and Caithness. Completed in 1869, but with no funding remaining for the planned twin spires, it was the first new cathedral built in Scotland since the Reformation and is the furthest north cathedral in mainland Britain.

In the background are the farms, fields and homes of Kinmylies ('Cinn a milidh': warrior's head) rising to the Leachkin ('An Leacainn': the hillside), while unseen in the distance are the glens and mountains of Wester Ross. Merrill's illustration captures a view of Inverness which has remained virtually unchanged since Victorian times.

2. **Alturlie:** Herring fishing in the Beauly Firth

Alturlie, a small 18th-century fishing hamlet with many of the fishermen's cottages still intact, sits on a point of land jutting into the Beauly Firth four miles to the east of Inverness, close to Allanfearn and just north of Culloden. To the west rears the Kessock Bridge, built in 1982, its sweeping elegance and its tall towers dominating the skyline and speeding the traffic past Inverness up and down the A9.

For centuries Alturlie made its livelihood from the booming Moray Firth herring trade, until overfishing led to the industry's decline in the 1950s. During the dark nights in the bay, the lights of the small drifters were clearly visible bobbing up and down in the unpredictable currents as the local fishermen hauled in their bulging nets. Today the lights belong to the luxury dinghies and yachts as they head back to the security of Inverness Marina.

Across the Firth sits Munlochy and the Black Isle, while towards the east are Ardersier and the now closed McDermott's oil rig construction yard which, at its most productive, created over 4,000 jobs in the early years of the Oil Boom. Slightly further along the coastal walk is the imposing garrison of Fort George, one of the three forts (the others being Fort William and Fort Augustus, after the Duke of Cumberland's forenames) built in and around the Great Glen in the aftermath of the 1745 Jacobite Rebellion.

The coastal and inland walks and views from Alturlie are bracingly enjoyable, and the birds, particularly ducks, and sea life are abundant. It's a pleasant, relatively undisturbed spot, ideal for fishing and sailing but still very close to the urban amenities of Inverness and Nairn.

3. **Beauly Priory:** 800-year-old holy ruins

The ruins of one of the oldest, most striking and historically important buildings in the Highlands can be found in the attractive inland village of Beauly, 12 miles west of Inverness on what was the main A9 North Road, now the A862. The village's name derives from either the Gaelic 'Beul Ath' (mouth of the ford) or from Mary Queen of Scots' French description 'Beau Lieu' (beautiful place).

However, the Valliscaulian Order of Burgundian monks, who occupied Beauly Priory from the 13th to 15th centuries, gave it the Latin name of 'Prioritus De Bello Loco' (priory of the lovely spot), so that could be its origin. Situated close to the River Beauly, the Priory was founded by King Alexander II, and after the Reformation it passed into the hands of the Lords of Lovat. Merrill's illustration shows the largest intact section, the standing south wall, which was part of a larger complex, evidence of which, including the tombs of the local MacKenzie Clan, still remains. At the entrance to the Priory there stands an 800-year-old elm tree, the oldest elm tree in Europe.

The ruins of this ancient building are carefully preserved under the management of Historic Scotland. The Priory is open to the public every day, and it provides an intriguing glimpse into a long-vanished period of Highland history.

4. **Bona Lighthouse:** Final stage of the Canal

One of Scotland's two inland lighthouses, Bona signals the start of the final section of the Caledonian Canal before it enters the Beauly Firth at Inverness. Built by Thomas Telford in 1815, Bona is close to Lochend on the A82 south of Inverness and the entrance to Loch Dochfour, where the serene grandeur of Loch Ness reaches its northern conclusion.

Telford's design was an unusually-shaped octagonal two-storey building, with a one-storey dwelling house attached. The original light shone from an upper-storey oriel window which faced Loch Ness to warn sailors of the impending canal. The lighthouse was operational for almost 200 years until in 2002 the newer electric lights, operated by British Waterways, were replaced by a marker beacon.

As a result, the building fell into disrepair, suffered weather damage and its jetty crumbled into the loch. In 2006 plans to redevelop Bona as a Visitors' Centre were blocked by local residents. In 2008 the then-MSP for the area, David Stewart, began to revive local interest in Bona's restoration. With the assistance of Scottish Heritage and Vivat Trust, and at a cost of around £500,000, the building is now fully renovated and Category B listed. It opened in early 2015 as a six-bedroom luxury holiday rental home. The view from the house is a splendid one, and it is encouraging that a unique part of the Highlands' architectural history has been renovated and preserved for the nation.

5. **Castle Stuart:** 17th-century Tower House

During the 14th century a new type of castle began to appear in Scotland: the tower house. This defensive structure was unique to Scotland and had little in common with the earlier 13th-century large-scale fortresses or Norman keeps which were then the norm throughout the country. Merrill's illustration of Castle Stuart (or 'Stewart', which was altered by Mary Queen of Scots to 'Stuart' to reflect her French upbringing) is a fine example of a typical medieval tower house.

Castle Stuart stands beside the Moray Firth about seven miles north-east of Inverness just off the A96 road to Nairn, and it directly faces the Black Isle. It is an E-plan tower-house, with two control towers linked by a central block. The land was granted by Mary Queen of Scots to James Stewart, the first Earl of Moray, in 1561. Both the first and second Earls were murdered, and the building was completed by the third Earl (James

Stuart) in 1625. After the execution of Charles I, the royalist Earls of Moray abandoned the castle, which then lay derelict for almost 300 years.

Castle Stuart was recently fully renovated by the Laird, Charles Stuart, over a 15-year period, with some of its furniture carved from 400-year-old oak. Stories and legends linger about mysterious deaths and haunted rooms, perhaps encouraged by the castle's somewhat architecturally forbidding appearance.

However, it is now an extremely comfortable, highly praised, eight-bedroom hotel, although it seems to retain a slightly edgy, almost eerie atmosphere. If you are of an over-imaginative, Gothic disposition, you can always go and play golf on the neighbouring Championship course. That'll calm you down.

6. **Cawdor Castle:** 'Flourish the Thorn'

Mention the name 'Cawdor' to many people, and it will almost certainly invoke memories of Shakespeare's play 'Macbeth', when one of the three witches proclaims to Macbeth: 'all hail to thee, Thane of Cawdor'. Fact and fiction, however, are not always reliable bedfellows. The 'real' King Macbeth died almost 150 years before such a Thaneship existed, and 300 years before the splendid Cawdor Castle was constructed. Indeed, the fifth Earl of Cawdor once said: 'I wish the Bard had never written his damned play.'

Cawdor Castle lies ten miles east of Inverness and five miles south-west of Nairn. The original castle was completed around 1454, although some of the stones have been dated to 1372, and it was home to the Clan Calder (hence 'Cawdor'). The building was taken over by the Clan Campbell in the 16th century and they remain owners.

This Category A listed tower house is a rectangular, four-storey building which had an entrance on the upper first floor to deter unwanted visitors. It was constructed around a holly tree (once believed to be a hawthorn, which existed in 1372) which can be seen in the dungeon. The Cawdor family toast is, appropriately, 'Flourish the Thorn!' The interior contains a large drawing room, portraits, tapestry bedroom, dining room and an old kitchen. Its gardens are highly regarded. The Walled Garden was created around 1600, the Flower Garden a century later, and the Wild Garden in the 1960s. There is also a wood containing over 100 species of lichen. Cawdor Castle is open to visitors from May to October.

7. **Chanonry Point:** Viewing bottlenose dolphins

Chanonry Point ('Gob Na Cananaich': point of the seashore) sits on the tip of Chanonry Ness, a spit of land which stretches into the Moray Firth between the Black Isle towns of Fortrose and Rosemarkie. Most of the land is occupied by Fortrose and Rosemarkie Golf Club, while just across the Firth are Fort George and Ardersier.

Merrill's illustration is of Chanonry Point Lighthouse with, in the background, the hills rising south-west of Inverness. The lighthouse was designed and built by Alan Stevenson, Robert Louis Stevenson's uncle, in 1846. Originally a 'one-man station', it is over 40 feet high, a white structure, with 48 steps to the tower and a range of 15 nautical miles. It was automated in 1984, and the adjacent accommodation is now privately owned. The lighthouse stands directly behind the green of the golf course's 4th hole.

The Point is one of the most accessible and popular spots in Britain to view the bottlenose dolphin, of which there are around 130 living in the Firth. The optimum time of day to observe these soaring silvery mammals is at low tide, when the salmon, on which the dolphins largely feed, are returning across the Firth to the Rivers Ness and Beauly. Around the Point there are also grey seals, frolicking porpoises, occasional otters and a variety of unusual bird life. However, unfortunately you will not be able to see the Highland prophet, the Brahan Seer, who was burnt alive in the 17th century in a barrel of burning oil on what is now the golf club. Nevertheless, the views in all directions from Chanonry Point are stunning.

8. **Clachnaharry:** Canal meets the Firth

The Caledonian Canal enters the Beauly Firth through a sea lock at Clachnaharry, an old fishing village which marks the western boundary of the city of Inverness. Merrill's drawing is a view from the A862 road from Beauly (the A9 as was, before the usurpation of this roadway by the Kessock Bridge) just before it enters the city. The illustration focuses on the narrow projection of land, reminiscent of a jetty, surrounding the canal's exit, while, across the Beauly Firth, slope the fertile hills of the southern Black Isle.

Clachnaharry is located two miles from the city centre, and takes its name from 'Clach na h-Aithrigh', the Gaelic for 'stone of repentance'. The name refers either to a bloody battle fought here in 1454 between the Clans Munro and Chattan (a ruined nearby memorial commemorates the battle) or the end of a massive pub crawl which started at the eastern end of the city and terminated here. The former explanation is more likely.

The old railway station at Clachnaharry closed in 1913. The centre of the hamlet today is the welcoming old ex-coach house, the Clachnaharry Inn, established in 1836, which offers fine beer and food and a beer garden which sits by the edge of the railway line. On a clear day, there are superb views over the mountains to the north and west of Inverness, and also, to the east, the Kessock Bridge and beyond.

9. **Clava Cairns:** Bronze Age chamber tombs

One of Scotland's best-preserved prehistoric burial sites is located one mile south-east of Culloden battlefield. The Clava Cairns - or, to be more precise, the 'Balnuaran of Clava' - lie close to the River Nairn and are today overshadowed by the towering Culloden Viaduct.

The Cairns site consists of three Bronze Age stone burial chambers, each enclosed by standing stone circles, which were built approximately 4,000 years ago. In this Late Neolithic period, ancestor worship was of considerable cultural significance, and the size of these chambers suggest they were the last resting places of high priests or tribal chieftains.

The two outer chambers of the Clava Cairns are of the 'passage grave' type, where a single burial chamber was linked to an entrance by a short, 10-feet high passageway (today worn down to around three feet). The central chamber is of the 'ring cairn' type, which had no access to the outside world and normally contained a single body. The stones are carved with 'cup and ring' marks, symbols of fertility, and they are oriented in a north-east to south-west direction towards the mid-winter sunset, suggesting a sun-worshipping culture. This possibility is emphasised by the increasing size of the stones as they approach the south-west corner of the site.

There are several other examples in this area of this form of cairn construction, but none of the others retains the detailed stonework and scenic grandeur of the Clava Cairns, nor enjoys the peaceful setting of the woodland which surrounds these mysterious tombs. The Clava Cairns remain as a memorial and tribute to the culture and beliefs of the ancient inhabitants of the Highlands.

10. **Clock Tower:** 18th-century Inverness clock

Shortly after the Parliamentarian victory over the Royalist forces in the 17th-century War of the Three Kingdoms, Oliver Cromwell set about attempting to impose order on the Highlands, an unenviable task.

Between 1652 and 1658 his men constructed a Citadel adjacent to the Harbour area of Inverness. This was a large, pentagonal structure, open to the River Ness on its western wall, which could hold a garrison of 1000 men. After the Restoration of King Charles II, the Citadel was demolished in 1662, with much of the stone eventually used to build a bridge over the river.

For many years it was generally believed that the Clock Tower, on today's Cromwell Road, had been part of Cromwell's fort. However, recent research revealed that the Tower was erected over a century later than had been supposed, and that it formed part of a rope and hemp factory constructed on the site of the old Citadel in the 1780s. Nevertheless, the Tower is the second-oldest building in Inverness, after the Old High Church.

The Tower is a virtually square-sided structure and is topped by a slated belfry and a weather-vane. There is a small doorway on the south-east side. The clock and bell are still in working order. The Tower was Category B listed in 1971 and it was thoroughly restored by the Inverness Common Good Fund in 2010.

Although its location today may not be in the most salubrious part of the city, the Clock Tower is a building of considerable historical interest and an integral part of the fabric of old Inverness.

11. **Culloden House:** Palladian country mansion

For 250 years, the Georgian mansion known as Culloden House has presided over its 40 acres of private woods and parklands just over four miles to the east of Inverness.

Originally a fortified castle, it was acquired in 1625 from the chief of Clan MacKintosh by the Forbes family, who became owners of the House for the following 300 years. In 1746 the building was requisitioned by Charles Edward Stuart prior to the Battle of Culloden three miles to the south and, after the Jacobite defeat, the victorious Duke of Cumberland briefly stayed here.

The then-owner, Duncan Forbes, was Lord President of the Scottish Court of Session and, although a committed Hanoverian, he pleaded for leniency for the Jacobite prisoners on trial in London. This humane action irritated the Government and they refused to pay for damage to his property, thereby ruining him financially.

The House was rebuilt between 1772 and 1778 to the design of Robert Adams, a friend of the family, whose influence is evident in its Palladian style. The main section of the House is a three-storey, high-ceilinged, spacious building, connected by screened walls on each side to two smaller Pavilions, which are built over the cellars of the original first floor of the former castle.

Culloden House is today a luxury four-star hotel with four public rooms, including a large drawing room, Adams plasterwork, a collection of antiques and a wide, open fireplace. The handsome exterior of the House confirms it as one of Scotland's leading country house mansions.

12. **Culloden Viaduct:** Elegance in Strathnairn

Soaring effortlessly over the wide valley of the River Nairn, the Culloden Viaduct is a peerless testament to the construction talent and technical skill, as well as the visionary optimism, of late-Victorian engineering. In my eyes, at least, the Viaduct is an architectural masterpiece, in terms of its scale, seductively curving silhouette and virtually seamless absorption into its natural backdrop of Strathnairn. It is, indeed, a thing of wonder.

The Viaduct was designed by Murdoch Paterson for the Highland Main Line Railway. It was opened in 1898 and today it remains, at 1800 feet in length, the largest masonry viaduct in Scotland. Paterson considered the Viaduct his greatest achievement although he died before the Viaduct was completed.

The Category A listed, double-track Viaduct is built from red sandstone and contains 29 arches, all 50 feet in length apart from the 100-feet span over the river, with a grassy northern end and a southern end supported by thousands of tonnes of hardcore and rock as a support against landslides. Culloden Moor station was located at the northern end until its closure in the 1960s. This architectural gem is also known as the 'Nairn' or 'Clava' Viaduct and is located six miles east of Inverness, the Line's terminus.

On the occasions when I used to travel on the overnight London to Inverness sleeper, the guard always made a point before the train reached the Viaduct of waking passengers so they could take in the spectacular views, particularly to the north. I find it difficult to conceive of a more stunning and original introduction to the Highlands than entering the region by way of the Culloden Viaduct.

14. **Dulsie Bridge:** Spanning Findhorn Gorge

One of Scotland's longest rivers, the Findhorn, meanders and tumbles its 65-mile journey from the Monadhliath Mountains to the Moray Firth. Some 12 miles to the south-east of Nairn the river enters a deep gorge and surges under the granite-built, 260-year-old, Category A listed Dulsie Bridge.

The bridge was built in 1755, under the supervision of Major William Caufield, to carry a military road from Braemar to Fort George as part of the Hanoverian government's attempts to 'pacify' the Highlands after the 1745 Rebellion. There is no doubt that it is an impressive and well preserved structure. It is a double arched, single span bridge, with its parapet 60 feet above the river's normal summer level, and is not far short of 50 feet in length. As can be seen from Merrill's illustration, the rock on one side is slightly higher than on the other, giving it a slanted appearance.

As one can imagine, the river, one of the finest in Scotland for salmon fishing, is popular at this stage with canoeists and proponents of white water kayaking and rafting. Recently, the bridge has also been used by enthusiasts of 'tombstoning', which involves jumping off the bridge in a vertically straight line into the swirling water: to me, a pointless and dangerous activity but I guess I'm just getting old.

In 1787 Rabbie Burns stayed at the King's House Inn near the bridge and wrote 'Come through mist and darkness to Dulsie to lie, Findhorn River, rocky banks', which doesn't sound much like Burns but perhaps he had a bad night. However, a visit to Dulsie Bridge is certainly worth the minor inconvenience incurred in getting there.

14. **Dunlichity Church:** Ancient Christian worship

Although many of Merrill's illustrations in this book concern the city of Inverness, there are several which are some distance away. These include, to the south-east, Clava Cairns and the Culloden Viaduct and, to the south-west, Dores and Urquhart Castle. Here, the illustration - Dunlichity Church - is directly south of the city in the heart of Strathnairn, with Loch Ness to the west and the A9 main road to the north-east.

The name 'Dunlichity' is translated from the Gaelic as either 'Dun Fhluich Aite' (fort of the wet place) or 'Dunleeatti' (hill of the Catti), the latter being a reference to the ancestors of the Clan Chattan who controlled these lands and who ruled over several other clans, such as MacIntosh and MacGillivray.

Dunlichity Church has been part of the parish of Daviot since 1618 and lies around eight miles from Inverness. Merrill's illustration portrays the Category B listed church and graveyard from the east. This is the third church to have occupied this ancient site, with the original church dedicated to St Finan, Bishop of Lindisfarne, who preached here in the 7th century. During the Reformation in 1643 an effigy of Finan was taken from the church and burnt at Inverness Mercat Cross.

The current church was rebuilt in 1758, with space for a congregation of 300, and repaired in 1826 and 1859. Its relics include a handbell dating to 1702, and its walls are marked where arrows and swords were sharpened, ready for battle. The graveyard contains a Watch House built in 1820 for guarding the graves, which include walled enclosures for the local MacGillivrays and the Shaws. Close by on a hillside is the area's original baptismal stone.

There are several hidden-away, fascinating buildings surrounding Inverness, and Dunlichity Church is a typical example of this area's largely forgotten history.

15. **Eastgate Centre Clock:** Inverness surreal clock

For much of the 20th century Eastgate comprised a number of small shops and bars which gradually petered out in an easterly direction past Hamilton's Auction Mart and joining Millburn Road. This cosy facade faded away in 1983 with the opening of Phase 1 of the Eastgate Shopping Centre, and had disappeared by 2003 when Phase 2 was completed. Eastgate became and today remains the heart of the largest shopping catchment area in Europe.

Inevitably, there were casualties incurred in the creation of this temple to consumerism, in particular the Mart, the railway goods yard and the Lochgorm Works, but the reconfiguration of the city centre witnessed some interesting developments. One of these was the installation of the Eastgate Clock, as depicted in Merrill's illustration.

Donated at a cost of £10,000 by local Rotarian clubs in 2007 to mark their centenary, the clock has become something of a tourist attraction. It is a large, animated construction, designed by Aberdeen sculptor and designer Syd Burnett and built by Cumbria Clocks, responsible for public clocks in, among other locations, Hampton Court and Salisbury Cathedral.

Its metal figures and lighting effects represent Noah's Ark, and on the hour a monkey scales a tree and chimes a bell. The diorama then plays an animal-themed song while a single set of doors opens to reveal the animals associated with the song. At noon every day, the clock stages a five-minute-long dramatic performance, with all the animal doors opening and closing, to appropriate musical accompaniment and gasps of wonder from the surrounding kiddies.

This surreal horological timepiece is an unusual but welcome addition to public art in Inverness.

16. **Eden Court:** Cultural heart of the Highlands

One of the finest, best-equipped and most comprehensive arts and entertainment venues in Scotland sits close to the west bank of the River Ness, only a few minutes' pleasant stroll from the centre of Inverness.

Now including the Bishop's Palace, built in the 1870s as a formal residence for Robert Eden, the Bishop of Moray, Eden Court was unveiled in 1976 and became the town's only theatre, as the Empire had been demolished in 1971 and the Theatre Royal had burnt down in 1939. Its original glass design immediately caught the imagination of the public. By the early 21st century, however, it was clear that the Centre was increasingly inadequate for purpose and in need of major attention.

After a two-year closure a completely refurbished and significantly extended Eden Court reopened in 2007. The new complex includes a second theatre, two cinema screens (named La Scala and Playhouse in homage to the city's popular but departed cinemas), two performance and dance studios, a revamped restaurant and bar, three floors of purpose-built dressing rooms, a new entrance opening onto landscaped grounds (as Merrill's drawing illustrates) and essential structural improvements. Also, the Bishop's Palace and the first theatre were both Category A listed.

Eden Court is today indisputably the cultural centre of the Highland region. It stages operatic performances, modern and classical music concerts, theatre and drama, ballet and modern dance, contemporary and vintage film screenings, comedy evenings and an annual pantomime, and contains workshop rooms, conference facilities, and a great deal more.

As the city of Inverness continues to expand and embrace the modernity it has experienced in recent years, its cultural diversity and artistic vision will also grow and develop, as expressed in the admirable Eden Court Centre.

17. **Falcon Square:** Inverness public piazza

In 1855 the railway arrived in Inverness, the town becoming the western terminus of the Inverness and Nairn Railway. Over the following years as the geographical reach of the railway expanded, it set in motion profound changes in the cultural and commercial life of the town.

Much of the land adjacent to the station was soon occupied by the wholesale trade and by light industry, particularly around Falcon Square which was named after the Falcon Foundry, established close to the back of the old Station Hotel in 1858 by John Falconer but which ceased operation in the late 19th century.

When the Eastgate Centre opened in 1983, most of the foundry building had fallen into disrepair but an intact section remained and was awarded Category B listing as one of the few buildings left from the town's Victorian past. Several years later, as part of the Phase II expansion of the Centre, this listed building was dismantled brick by brick and rebuilt at a 90-degree angle to its former position. The new Falcon Square opened in 2003.

Merrill's illustration portrays a view of Falcon Square as it is today, seen from Millburn Road. The old foundry building, now occupied by Laura Ashley and Pizza Express, is to the left, the rear of the old Station Hotel and the roof of the station in the centre, and the new Eastgate extension on the right. Not included in the scope of Merrill's illustration is the new 'Mercat Cross', erected in 2003 and which features a rearing unicorn on top of a 37-feet-high sandstone pillar. Falcon Square is now Inverness's main public square and piazza, and the principal gathering point for a variety of private and civic events.

18. **Falls of Foyers:** Plunging into Loch Ness

'Among the heathy hills and ragged woods
The roaring Foyers pours his mossy floods'

So wrote Rabbie Burns in 1787 ('with a pencil on the spot') as he contemplated the Falls of Foyers.

The village of Foyers sits above Loch Ness on the eastern side of the loch, roughly halfway between Dores and Fort Augustus. Less popular with travellers than the lochside western stretch between Inverness and Fort Augustus, the B852 was built by General Wade after the 1715 Jacobite Rebellion. It was, however, used mainly by Prince Charlie and his men as they tramped their way south in 1745.

The Falls of Foyers is one of the most dramatic sights in the Highlands. Falling a total of 165 feet almost vertically into a dark, foaming pool and then through a gorge into the loch, the Falls has been a tourist attraction since Victorian days when visitors travelled from Inverness on a paddle steamer to visit the waterfall. Today, more modern vessels take a similar route.

Known in Gaelic as 'Eas na Smuide' (smoking falls), the Falls celebrates the climax of the River Foyers, which tumbles down from the Monadhliath Mountains. The surging power of the river at Foyers was first harnessed in 1896 in order to provide hydroelectricity for the aluminium works, which closed in 1967, hence the relatively large size of the village.

The visitor negotiates a steep path down a forested slope to reach the best observation point from which to observe the swirling water as it squeezes its way through a narrow opening to launch its vertiginous, majestic plunge to its resting place in Loch Ness. Its widening trajectory and the powerful energy of the waterfall is well illustrated by Merrill's drawing, as observed from the west close to Loch Ness.

19. **Inverness Castle:** Grandiose Victorian landmark

When looking across the Inverness skyline, it is almost impossible to miss the pinkish-red towers and turrets of Inverness Castle, standing on a hill above the River Ness and the streets of the old town centre.

Merrill's illustration shows the castle as seen from the western bank of the river. To the castle's right stands the Burgh Steeple at the corner of Bridge and Church Streets, built in 1791 and once the town Tollbooth. Guarding the main entrance to the castle's left is the brass statue of Flora MacDonald peering down the river, perhaps expectantly awaiting the return of Charles Edward Stuart.

The castle, built in 1836 and considered by some observers to be a Victorian 'folly' and an egregious example of 'Highlandism', is only one of several castles to have occupied this strategically important position. In the 12th century King David I built an earth and timber fortress which was destroyed by Robert the Bruce in the 14th century. The Clans Donald and MacKintosh then interchanged ownership. The 15th century saw the erection by the Earl of Mar of a stone castle, which was then occupied by the Earl of Huntly until Mary Queen of Scots kicked him out after she laid siege to the building in 1562. It changed hands during the War of the Three Kingdoms, was taken over by General Wade after 1715, and then blown up by Prince Charlie in 1746. It has certainly had an intriguing history.

The castle is today used as a courthouse, among other things, and there is currently much discussion over its most appropriate usage. However, whatever one's opinion on the architectural merits of the building and its future function in the city, there is little doubt that the views from the hill, particularly up to the Ness Islands and beyond to the Great Glen, are magnificent.

20. **Jacobite Queen:** Cruising Loch Ness

The splendour of the Great Glen and in particular Loch Ness is, appropriately, best appreciated by boat. Tourist steamers have journeyed round the loch since Victorian times. However, the creation of Jacobite Cruises in 1975 established the first return trips up the Caledonian Canal from Inverness to the loch in a comfortable environment with a guided commentary and a regular timetable.

Today, Jacobite Cruises, the largest such company on the loch, operates four vessels from its starting points of Tomnahurich Bridge, where the A82 Fort Augustus Road crosses the Caledonian Canal, and from a more recent departure point established at Dochgarroch Lock further up the Canal towards the loch. The company flagship is the *Jacobite Queen*, shown in Merrill's illustration on its way back to Inverness at the end of the loch, with Tor Wood and Dores to its right, and approaching Aldourie and journey's end.

The *Jacobite Queen* operates two daily return cruises from Tomnahurich to the ruins of Urquhart Castle near Drumnadrochit, each trip lasting two hours. Built in 1949, the boat was originally a passenger ferry on the River Tyne until it was bought by Jacobite, overhauled and refitted, and it began running trips on the loch in 1987. Almost 70 feet in length, the vessel has room for 159 passengers and three crew members.

Although the countryside before Dochgarroch is rather lacking in visual interest, thereafter you enter some of the most arresting scenery anywhere in the world, as the *Jacobite Queen* approaches the northern tip of Loch Ness and heads south-west to Urquhart Castle.

Dwarfed by the steep sloping hills of the Great Glen, and powering through one of the largest expanses of freshwater anywhere in the British Isles, the *Jacobite Queen* offers a joyous insight into the rugged beauty of the Highland landscape.

21. **Kessock Bridge:** Soaring across the Beauly Firth

Various ferries have connected North and South Kessock since at least the 15th century. However, perhaps for financial or engineering reasons, no one appears to have considered bridging the Beauly Firth at this particular point until the Kessock Bridge opened in 1982.

Merrill's illustration well portrays the sweep of the bridge from the Inverness shore of the Firth, just north of the Caley Thistle stadium, to the Black Isle in the background. For the technically-minded, this is a cable-stayed structure with a length of 3465 feet and a span of 787 feet. It's held in place by four 150-feet-high bridge towers and is tall enough to allow ships into Inverness harbour. Apparently, its design is based on a bridge over the Rhine near Düsseldorf. For the rest of us non-techies, it cuts over 20 miles off the old, lengthy and time-consuming A9 via Beauly, it exists in pleasing unity with its environment, and it means you don't have to drive through Inverness any more.

In 2014 Transport for Scotland invested £13 million in refurbishing and updating the structure. It was originally built as the first phase in the northern redevelopment of the A9, avoiding the previous detours around the Beauly, Cromarty and Dornoch Firths, a project completed in 1991 with the concrete Tain to Dornoch raised carriageway.

The streamlined contours and harmonious design of Kessock Bridge can perhaps be seen as yet another totemic metaphor for Inverness's surge in recent years from a relatively sleepy Highland town to one of Europe's fastest-growing cities. Or maybe it's just a bridge.

22. **Leanach Cottage:** Survivor of Culloden carnage

'Field of the English. They were buried here.' All fifty of them. If you compare this figure to the estimated 1500 Jacobites killed during or shortly after the hour-long Battle of Culloden on 15 April 1746, then you will understand that this, the last battle fought on British soil, was a massacre.

The above motif is carved on one of the many commemorative stones which today remain, askew and desolate, on Drumossie Moor, four miles south-east of Inverness. Known as 'The English Stone', this memorial to the dead of the Hanoverian forces stands just to the west of Old Leanach Cottage, the only building on the battlefield to remain virtually intact during the savage rout of the many men courageously but fatally loyal to Charles Edward Stuart.

The original, small, turf-walled cottage lay behind the Hanoverian lines, untroubled by the Jacobites, and was probably used as a field hospital by the Government army. Part of the 'ferm toun' of the Forbes of Culloden estate, the cottage was surrounded by barns, all razed to the ground by the victors. Around 30 wounded Jacobites were discovered hiding in one of the barns. The Hanoverians locked the doors and burned them alive.

The current Leanach Cottage, the small thatched roofed building in Merrill's illustration, dates from 1760. Standing close to the Culloden Visitors' Centre, it was inhabited until 1912, when it was donated to the Inverness Gaelic Society and restored to its pre-1745 interior. It has been owned and maintained by the National Trust for Scotland since 1944. It is difficult to suppress at least a tinge of melancholia when observing the austere bleakness of Leanach Cottage.

23. **Inverness Public Library:** Stately public building

As a kid growing up in 1960s Inverness I used to change my grannie's library books for her. They were usually romances featuring doctors called Hamish and nurses named Heather. If my grannie's initials weren't on the half-title page, then she hadn't read them, so in my bag they went. The library was then almost apologetically tucked away in Castle Wynd, an afterthought behind the architectural disaster that was the new Bridge Street. It was not an impressive public library. So it was with a glad heart that, after some time away from the town, I discovered the new library location in Farraline Park.

Built in 1841 as a Bell's Institution school, and then used as a courthouse, police station and theatre, this handsome Greek-Revival style, Doric porticoed, square-stoned structure, as detailed in Merrill's illustration, was much more like a proper library, which it became in 1980. Its position facing Inverness's main bus station detracts slightly from its deserved lofty prominence in the square, but

anything is better than Castle Wynd. In 2011 the library was absorbed into High Life Highland, a Highland Council cultural initiative.

As well as innumerable shelves of books, and walls boasting oil portraits of Victorian Invernessians, the library offers in-house and online catalogues containing magazines, newspapers, pamphlets and much more, dating back to the early 19th century, if not earlier. As I discovered to my pleasure, it also has a fine collection of volumes on Inverness.

As with most British libraries, there is not enough available space for their collections (in the case of Inverness, only half the room they require). There has also recently been talk about moving the library again and turning Farraline Park into an open public square. However, it would be a shame to lose that worthy facade, a welcoming entrance to an invaluable public resource.

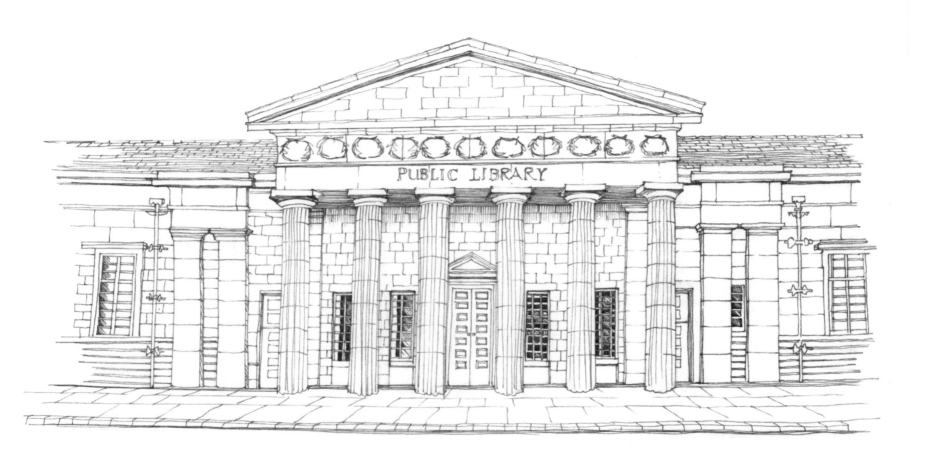

24. **Loch Ness from Dores:** Stunning scenery

The final stretch of the nine-mile journey south-west from Inverness to Dores brings to mind GK Chesterton's line 'the rolling English road'. 'Rolling' is as good a description as any, with the road's narrow, hilly contours revealing the approaching Loch Ness. Furthermore, the original road was constructed by an Englishman, General Wade, after the 1715 Jacobite Rebellion.

Dores (from the Gaelic 'duras', meaning 'black wood') is a small hamlet of houses, a Parish Hall and the justifiably renowned Dores Inn. It is a place where very little seems to have happened over the centuries, unless one includes the recent annual Rockness music festival, now cancelled.

However, Dores perches on the north-eastern corner of Loch Ness and is fortunate to possess arguably the finest view in the Highlands. Merrill's evocative drawing illustrates the remaining wooden stanchions of the old steamer jetty at the rear of the Dores Inn, while beyond these into the distance unfolds the wide expanse of the 22-mile loch, overseen by the surrounding, brooding forested hills.

By coincidence the tree in the foreground casts its shadow over the spot on which I used to pitch my tent on my regular youthful camping trips. The shoreline is only yards away but, given the icy nature of the loch, I suggest you go no further and that you certainly resist the temptation to go for a swim.

However, to stand on the pebble beach and contemplate the deceptively tranquil solemnity of the loch is, curiously, an experience to raise the spirits and enliven the mood of even the most cynical. On the western bank lie the inlets of Drumnadrochit and Invermoriston, while along Glen Mhor to the east sit Inverfarigaig and Foyers before the road veers up to the lochs and moorland of Stratherrick and finally joins its busier companion at the abbey village of Fort Augustus.

25. **Market Brae Steps:** Eastgate to the Crown

Many visitors to Inverness may be unaware of the attractions of the essentially residential Crown area. However, there are fine views of the city and beyond to be enjoyed from here if you are prepared to tackle the uphill stepped braes.

The two main sets of steps leading from the city centre to the Crown are the Raining Stairs on Castle Street and the Market Brae, diagonally across from the Eastgate Centre. The latter is wider and less steep than the former, and there are shops and other commercial outlets to maintain one's interest while navigating the Market Brae. The Stairs and the Steps are only a few yards apart when they both emerge close to Ardconnel Street which, at its southern end, passes Porterfield Prison to connect with the top of Castle Hill.

Merrill's illustration details the top entrance to the Market Brae Steps with the north of the city in the distance. In order to reach this spot, one zig-zags

one's way past, among others, hair, nail and bridal gown shops, a kilt-maker and other small traders and businesses.

Behind this observation point, and to one's right, is Ardconnel Terrace, which loops round the peak of the hill and from which the distant Moray Firth and Black Isle are clearly visible. The road concludes at the junction with Stephens Brae opposite the currently unoccupied old Royal Academy building, with the shops of Kingsmills only a five-minute walk away.

As you stroll shopwards, the residential grid structure of the Charles Street, Crown Street and Hill Street area is to your right, while in the opposite eastern direction, and ahead of you, are the bourgeois, larger houses of the Crown. It's a quiet, peaceful area of Inverness for an amble around, and worth an expedition up the Market Steps.

MARKET BRAE STEPS

26. **Ness Islands:** Relaxation in Inverness

Nestling unobtrusively to the south-west of the city, the Ness Islands have provided a secluded retreat for Invernessians since early Victorian times.

Positioned at one of the River Ness's narrowest points, just below the river's most convenient natural ford, and bounded by the Bught Park to the west and what is now Island Bank Road to the east, their only means of access was by boat until bridges were built to each bank in 1829 and 1834.

The great flood of 1849, which swept away the main seven-arched stone bridge in the town centre, also demolished these Islands bridges. They were replaced in 1854 by suspension bridges, as seen in Merrill's illustration, and a beam bridge connects the two larger Islands. Flooding remains a continual worry for today's owners, the Inverness Common Good Fund, as does high wind damage to the trees, so on occasion the Islands have to be closed to the public for safety reasons. However, in 2015 Highland Council approved a three-year updating management plan for this relaxing public amenity.

The Islands' pathways are shaded by imported Scots pine, fir, beech and sycamore, and there is a variety of unusual wild and bird life and abundant salmon and hopeful anglers. As well as providing scope for peaceful promenades, the Islands have been home to an open air auditorium, tea rooms and, in the 1960s, a popular roller-skating rink, all now gone.

Close by, entertainments include the Bught Park football pitches and the late-1960s Ice Rink, and in Whin Park there are children's play facilities and the UK's most northerly small-gauge mini-railway, with three locomotives providing trips of up to half a mile. However, the essence of the Ness Islands is calmness and serenity, perfectly captured in Merrill's illustration.

27. **Norbord Factory:** Nostalgic steam plume

'Is that the place they make clouds, Mum?' If any of your young children ask you this when you're driving along the A96 Inverness to Nairn road, then you are far from alone. The Norbord factory, close to the turn-off for Dalcross Airport, would undoubtedly be missed if it ceased production as, for over thirty years, the seemingly permanent funnel of steam issuing from the works has become a landmark on the journey.

Norboard is an international company, manufacturing wood-based panel products, MDF and flat pack furniture. Admittedly, one would not expect to come across an illustration of a factory in a book which celebrates the history and culture of the Inverness area. Norbord, however, is an exception and a local institution due to its durability and, strangely enough, its incongruity.

Surrounded by the forests, fields and farms of its agricultural environment, its endless column of steam drifts over the flat border country where Inverness-shire meets Nairnshire. It must be, for a visitor, an unexpected sight, but Merrill's decision to include it in this volume is an entirely understandable one.

Like many other Invernessians, I consider Norbord as integral a part of Inverness as are Eden Court, the Kessock Bridge and the Eastgate Centre, all of which are included without equivocation in this volume. 'History' is as much about a sense of belonging and identity as it is about tradition, and Norbord well satisfies the former criteria.

It was heartening to read in November 2014 that Highland Council have approved Norbord's expansion plans. When I return to Inverness via Dalcross, I feel that the plume is almost welcoming me home, a sentiment I am sure I share with many other exiles.

28. **Old Royal Academy:** 20th-century education

The Victorian building represented in Merrill's illustration is the frontage of the old Inverness Royal Academy at the top of Stephens Brae, drawn from a position just inside the entrance gates. I should know this, as I was a pupil at the school between 1963 and 1968 and stood here often enough.

The first Grammar School in the town was established by Dominican Friars in 1223, followed by the Town Grammar School in 1688. The original Royal Academy was opened in Academy Street in 1792 as a 'seminary for young gentlemen' although girls were admitted from the outset. The school moved uphill to the Crown area in 1895 and remained there, with various additions and alterations, for almost 85 years. It stopped being an independent school in 1908, and its fee-paying status disappeared with the 1945 Education Act. In 1979 it moved to its present location in Culduthel,

leaving its 4.2 acre Crown site in the care of the University of the Highlands and Islands.

The school was mainly laid out alongside Midmills Road, and was where the gym and the newer buildings, including the spacious, bright assembly hall, were located. The earlier classrooms were Victorian in design with their high ceilings and large windows and high sills and, on the upper floor, several doors opened onto a walkway surrounding an open-topped library, the core of the building.

Like most Scottish schools, Inverness Royal was a disciplinarian establishment but it was highly respected in both the academic and sporting spheres. The site was put up for sale at the end of 2014. One hopes that whoever buys it affords the building the care and attention which the old place deserves.

29. **Old High Church:** Inverness Parish Church

After stepping down from the Greig Street suspension bridge onto Bank Street on the east side of the River Ness, one is confronted by two churches. On the right is the gloomy exterior of the Free Church of Scotland, while to the left is a jumbled old graveyard, behind which sits the Old High Church: the town Parish Church and the oldest place of Christian worship in Inverness.

In its time, the Old High, accessed via Church Street, which is one of the oldest streets in Inverness, has been claimed by Celtic, Roman Catholic, Episcopalian and, as it is today, Presbyterian doctrines. In the 6th century AD, St Columba used St Michael's Mound, on which the Category A listed Old High still stands, to preach Christianity to King Brude and the Picts.

The tower, which can be seen in Merrill's illustration as viewed from the river, dates from the 16th century, although the lower stonework is probably from an earlier period. The parapet and spire belong to the 18th century. It used to be known as 'The English Church' as the Gaelic tongue was not used in its services. Its 'English' identity was reinforced after the Battle of Culloden when Jacobite prisoners were briefly imprisoned in the church, taken outside to the graveyard and shot dead.

The building was urgently in need of repair by the mid-18th century, so it was largely rebuilt in 1770 with sufficient capacity in its three galleries and apse for a congregation of over 1800 worshippers. It was refurbished in 1891 and re-roofed in 1898. The Old High Church tower appears prominently in many of the paintings and drawings of medieval and old Inverness, demonstrating its pivotal pastoral importance in the history of the town.

30. **Phoenix Ale House:** Best bar in Inverness

Inverness is a thirsty place, a fact reflected in the number of bars which grace the city. In recent years gentrification and modernisation has seen the emergence of several splendid drinking venues but the same inexorable process has led to the lamentable disappearance of many others: Haugh, Lochiel, Argyle, Lochgorm, Northern, Citadel, Albert... I would continue but for the tears blurring my vision.

It is, therefore, encouraging to see the continuing good health and, indeed, refurbishment, of a bar which has always been one of Inverness's most interesting and inclusive drinking dens: The Phoenix. The bar, which occupies the junction of Rose Street and Academy Street, was granted a public house licence in 1846, and it is, along with the Gellions, one of Inverness's oldest bars. It was recently reborn as The Phoenix Ale House.

Under the ownership of the redoubtable George MacLean, the pub has been smartened up (but not too much) and the oval bar remains encircled at its base by an original glazed Terrazzo spitoon. It also retains an old beer pump powered by water pressure. Otherwise, all the bar equipment and much else has been updated and modernised.

As one can observe from Merrill's illustration, the facade of the Phoenix is an attractive and inviting one. The old function room remains, with its mural of old Highland characters who drank and caroused in the bar, and there is also a restaurant with its own lounge bar.

The Phoenix carries a wide, well-researched range of real ales and malt whiskies, and the clientele continues to be a diverse one, with journalists, brickies, postmen, office workers and all sorts getting along just fine, drinking, arguing or watching football on the TV. The Phoenix is, to my mind, by some degree the finest bar in Inverness.

31. **Raining Stairs:** Steep climb to the Crown

The Raining Stairs is far from being the most seductively charming of Inverness's many attractions. In fact, you could describe it as a dishevelled narrow path from the Crown down to the city centre, and it is very steep, dangerously so if you've had a few at the Heathmount. You need to watch your step, particularly at night, as you descend this alleyway, although in 2014 it was given a £20,000 facelift by the Council which perked it up and much improved its appearance and safety level.

However, as Merrill's illustration makes clear, the view from the top takes in the Castle, the Town House at the bottom and the distant hillsides of the Leachkin, so it's a pleasing prospect. The Stairs has become an almost dignified local institution, so it's well worthy of inclusion in this volume.

Its name derives from the old Raining School, a solid, three-storey Georgian building which was funded by Scottish merchant John Raining of Norwich and which opened in 1757 under the strict control of the Society for the Propagation of Christian Knowledge. The school stood at the top of the Stairs just off Ardconnel Street and it closed in 1894 when its pupils moved to the High School.

The building remained in place, however, and was used for a variety of purposes, including a kindergarten, a YWCA, a 1950s rock 'n roll venue called the 50/50 Club and a 1960s 'youth club' named Doc Hay's Club (but known as the Doc's Club) where a bunch of largely teenage tearaways, myself included, stumbled around to the music of such local bands as The Flock and Size Four. That's all gone now, but the Raining Stairs remains a handy shortcut for reaching the smart cafes and shops of Castle Street and beyond.

32. **Reelig Glen:** Tallest conifers in Britain

Forests are rarely regarded as scenic attractions by visitors to the Highlands. Dark mountains, mysterious lochs, rugged coastal cliffs, rushing rivers, heather moorlands... these are the stuff of romantic Highland dreams. But trees?

A visit to Reelig Glen, however, will certainly change one's attitude. A journey of around seven miles on the A862 from Inverness towards Beauly and a left turn for Moniack will bring you to a car park. Climb the hill through 'The Cathedral', a planting of old beech trees, and you will find yourself beside Moniack Burn in the sheltered, steep-sided gorge of Reelig Glen, an unusual area of conifer and broadleaved woodland.

On the path marked Tall Trees Walk, the owners of the Glen, the Forestry Commission, announced in 2002 the existence of a Douglas Fir, planted over 100 years ago, which was, at 200 feet high, the tallest tree in Britain. It was named 'Dughall Mhor:' Big Douglas. In 2014 they revealed an even taller Douglas Fir whose 217-feet height made it the tallest conifer in Europe. They also found Britain's tallest lime tree (151 feet) and larch tree (157 feet).

One of the slender, straight conifers from the Glen was felled to serve as a replacement mast for Robert Scott's ship 'Discovery' over 100 years ago. This magnificent grove of giant trees was planted by the Fraser family who owned the land before the Commission acquired it in 1949.

The walks through the Glen also reveal rare woodland plants, red squirrels and other native flora and fauna, and at the top of the Glen is a stone bridge and grotto called in Gaelic 'Tigh an Aigh': the 'Fairy Glen'. This unique little spot attracts 12,000 visitors annually, which says much about its appeal.

33. **River Ness:** The heart of Inverness

Inverness would not exist in anything like its current form without the River Ness and its estuary. The river has been of vital strategic and economic importance to the development of Inverness since at least Pictish times.

In her illustration, Merrill looks downstream from Ness Bank on the eastern side of the river with the narrow Infirmary Bridge and Islands behind her. Across the river is the Cathedral, and then Ardross Terrace leads to the 'new' concrete bridge, which in 1961 replaced the grand 100 year old suspension bridge.

The east bank is largely obscured by bushes until one views a section of the 'new' bridge and then the river curves round past the unmistakeable tower of the Old High Church. The backdrop is Ben Wyvis, from whose slopes originate the local phrase 'snow on the Ben' indicating the approach of winter. Unusually, in the illustration there are no anglers on this stretch of the river. Birds, fish and wildlife flourish on and around the river, partly because the Ness never freezes and also because of the water's pollution-free clarity.

Further down the river there are four other bridges before the Ness meets the Beauly Firth: the pedestrian Greig Street Suspension Bridge; the recently re-surfaced Friar's Bridge which carries the A82 and was previously Waterloo Bridge (affectionately known as the 'Black Bridge', which was first built in 1808 to join the town to Merkinch village); the Grant Street Bridge, linking Academy Street to the city's last remaining Highland League club, Clachnacuddin FC; and a replacement railway bridge built in 1990.

The river then drifts through a near-derelict harbour, until relatively recently one of the Moray Firth's busiest herring ports, opposite a shipbuilding area, its skills in demand for almost 1000 years. Finally, the River Ness discharges itself into the sea, Inverness successfully negotiated and its work done.

34. **Stephens Brae:** Curving up to Old Academy

As well as the Market Brae and the Raining Stairs, illustrated elsewhere in this book, there is at least one other popular route down from the Crown escarpment to the city centre, namely Stephens Brae.

The Brae is a steep, traffic-free street which doglegs its way down to one's left from the old Royal Academy to the Eastgate Centre, which can today be reached at the point of the dogleg by a walkway across Crown Drive. Merrill's illustration shows the bottom of the Brae from Eastgate, with the steps to the left which stop halfway up, the narrow street which widens the further up one climbs, and the terrace of small buildings on the right-hand side.

The stretch nearer the top huddles under Ardconnel Street and is devoid of buildings on the right, while opposite is a small parade of tenement-style housing before one arrives at Crown Avenue and the Old Royal Academy. From this spot there is a view across the north of the city towards the Kessock Bridge and the Black Isle.

The Brae is probably named after St Stephen, the first Christian martyr, a supposition reinforced by the attractive little St Stephen's Church, further along past Kingsmills on Southside Road, which shares its congregation with the Old High.

As the consumerist commercial centre of Inverness has moved eastward in recent years, several small businesses and, in particular, restaurants have kept pace and they can be seen on the illustration. My own memory is of Academy pupils making their halting way up the hill at lunchtimes, carrying bags of chips from the Eastgate chippie close to the foot of the Brae. This proliferation of restaurants certainly did not exist in those days on Stephens Brae.

35. **The Three Graces:** Return of the statues

Inverness has never really been a town to embrace street or public art, perhaps preferring its built and natural environment to reveal its artistic grandeur in a subtler manner.

However, the recent homecoming of The Three Graces (or Three Virtues as they were more commonly known) was a cause for public celebration. These are three angelic nine-foot-high stone statues - representing Faith, Hope and Charity - created by sculptor Andrew Davidson in the 1870s, which stood on the roof of Alexander Cameron's drapery store on the corner of Castle Street and High Street, the site of today's McDonald's, until the shop was demolished in 1955. They then languished, forlorn and forgotten, in a Council yard until 1961 when they were acquired by an Orcadian, Norris Wood, and shipped north to adorn his garden.

After Wood's death, and under pressure from the public and the Inverness Old Town Art project, the four-tonne statues were purchased by the Inverness Common Good Fund for £15,000, removed from Orkney and, after a public consultation and vote on their location, were re-erected in 2011 in Ness Bank Gardens, the Highland Council providing the plinth for this 20-feet-high tribute to these noble sentiments.

So the statue now stands beside the Ness Bank Church looking over the river, with Hope holding a bible, Charity an anchor and Faith proferring a goblet to a young cherub. Spiritually, it's a world away from the Eastgate Centre although more prosaically, along with Flora MacDonald on the Castle Hill, they recently sported Caley Thistle scarves before the Scottish Cup Final. Faith and Hope won the day, as our local team claimed their first major Scottish trophy.

36. **Tomnahurich:** Hill of the yew trees

Back when the world was young and before kilts were invented, Inverness fiddlers Farquhar Grant and Thomas Cumming left the old town at midnight, staggered westward on the oak bridge over the Ness, and were stopped by a small man in a red tammie and green breeches who invited them to a party. They entered a door in a hillside, found a crowd of folk dancing and singing, and played all night. The next morning they left, walked back into town, and discovered that everything had changed beyond their recognition. They had been at a fairy party and had stayed for one hundred years. Farquhar and Thomas looked at each other, and crumbled to dust.

There are other similar folk tales concerning Tomnahurich Hill as the abode of the supernatural, which is why it is known as 'the hill of the fairies' although the Gaelic translation for Tomnahurich ('Ton na h-iubraich') is 'hill of the yew trees'. This 200-feet high 'esker', or a ridge of post-glacial gravel, lies a mile west of the city centre. There used to be a horse-racing track around the base of the Hill but since 1864 it was used as a public cemetery. The available space ran out in 1995 and it is now maintained by Highland Council.

Merrill's illustration captures the view from the path beside Torvean golf course on the west bank of the Caledonian Canal, with the A82 swingbridge to the left, the old Bridge House across the Canal and Tomnahurich Hill rising in the centre. The starting point for Jacobite Cruises is just out of the picture to the right. The main entrance to the cemetery is closer towards Inverness on Glenurquhart Road.

It's a pleasant walk up the winding paths of the tree-lined Hill where, at the top, sits a splendid War Memorial, and from which the panoramic views are memorable.

37. **Town House:** Imposing Inverness building

Merrill's detailed, intricately drawn illustration of Inverness Town House well portrays the Victorian Gothic, or 'Flemish Baronial', style of this splendid building.

Officially opened in 1882, it exudes the civic pride so closely associated with this period, with its municipal solidity, imposing entrance and slender towers and turrets conveying a sense of optimism and purpose. The two-storey interior continues this grand vision: the wide staircase, portraits and sculptures, crystal candelabras and spacious Hall are designed to impress yet are curiously welcoming.

Indeed, one of the finest and most intimate concerts I have attended was in this Hall in the late 1960s, when the singer/guitarist Davy Graham enthralled the audience as if he was playing in a small folk club. This is the same building where David Lloyd George on 7 September 1921 led the first ever Cabinet meeting to be held outside London. It is a diverse space which manages successfully to combine the duties of a council chamber with the more relaxed ambience of a musical and artistic venue.

The original Town House was built in 1708 as the town residence of Lord Lovat, becoming the Burgh Town House in 1716. On the paved area in front of the House ('the Exchange') stood the Market Cross and the Clach-na-Cudainn (the stone used by washerwomen to clean their clothing in the Ness), both of which remain today.

It was the Town Council base until the Glenurquhart Road offices took over in the 1980s, and today this Category A listed building, owned by the Inverness Common Good Fund, hosts meetings, civil functions and marriages, receptions and music of all types. At present it is undergoing a three-year, £4 million overhaul but it remains the pre-eminent building in the city.

38. **University of the Highlands and Islands:** Further education

For 500 years the most northerly university in Scotland was to be found in Aberdeen. However, it had long been felt that the Highlands was deserving of its own university. To this end, the UHI Project was established in 1992, became the UHI Millennium Institute in 2001 and in 2011 was granted the full status of the University of the Highlands and Islands.

The Inverness executive office co-ordinates the work of 13 colleges and research institutions across the region and beyond - from Oban to Thurso and from Elgin to Stornoway - and has an enrolment of around 40,000 undergraduate, postgraduate and further education students. It offers a remarkably wide variety of subjects and courses, including Scotland's only degree in Golf Management and, in Balloch close to Inverness, the Scottish School of Forestry. The emphasis is on the culture and history of the region but it also has a strong presence in science, health and engineering.

For the 2015/16 academic year, a new UHI campus opened in Inverness, replacing the old Midmills and Longman sites. This strikingly modern campus, as depicted in Merrill's illustration, is located among 30 acres of open parkland, with an artificial lochan, to the east of the city and close to the A9 near Raigmore Hospital.

Given its proximity to the Hospital, one of its main buildings is, appropriately, the Centre for Health Science, while across the A9 is the Learning Resource Centre, the focus for the other teaching and research units on the campus. It has capacity for around 6,500 students.

Not so many years ago, school leavers and older residents of Inverness had to leave the town and head south for their further education needs. It is gratifying to know that, with the continuing expansion of UHI, this no longer need be the case.

39. **Urquhart Castle:** Great Glen sentinel

The rocky promontory jutting into the 600-feet-deep Loch Ness just a mile or so south of the sheltered village of Drumnadrochit contains the ruins of Urquhart Castle. Sitting some 15 miles south of Inverness on the western bank of the loch, the brooding, ancient castle presents a stark contrast to the touristic, increasingly 'Nessie'-obsessed Drum.

The building was once the largest stone castle in the Inverness area and one of the largest in Scotland. Originally a 6th-century Pictish residence, by the 8th century it had become a Pictish 'broch' (a round inhabited tower). By the early 13th century it had been fortified by King Alexander II, who recognised its strategic importance in guarding the Great Glen route, and it was known as 'Caisteal na Sroin' (the fort of the promontory).

By the Wars of Independence, Urquhart Castle had been strengthened and enlarged, including the installation of a water gate onto Loch Ness. It was occupied by the English in 1296, recaptured by the Scots and besieged and overwhelmed by Edward I in 1303 but again recaptured by the Scots in 1308. The new Lords of Glenurquhart, the Clan Grant, added a five-storey tower house structure in 1509. The Grants withstood a blockade by Jacobite forces in 1689, but the castle was finally allowed to fall into ruin in 1692. Merrill's illustration views the castle from the north of Urquhart Bay, with Drumnadrochit off picture to the right.

Urquhart Castle is today officially classified as an Ancient Monument and is popular with visitors. A new car park was opened in 2002 and, among other attractions, there are an exhibition centre and a fascinating audio-visual exhibition. There is much more to Loch Ness than the Monster.

40. **Victorian Market:** Inverness covered mall

There was a long tradition of outdoor street markets in Inverness, but the widespread availability of gas-lighting in the 19th century meant that market shopping became a less chilly and more comfortable experience when enjoyed indoors.

In 1870 Inverness Town Council built a covered market in the centre of town but it was destroyed by fire in 1888. Undaunted, the Council rebuilt the Market in 1891, and it's still here today. The main entrance is on Academy Street, almost directly opposite the railway station, while the other means of access to this Victorian mall are on Union Street, Church Street and Queensgate. The Academy Street entry point is the original 1870 sandstone entrance, which has three round arches with a bull's head above the largest central arch and rams' heads on the smaller two.

Merrill's illustration is viewed from this entrance. One can see the two side lanes, the Market Clock,

the round-headed small shop fronts and the cast-iron, wooden-domed roof which lets in the light. Some of the Church Street sandstone arch has been worn away over the years by fishmongers who used it to sharpen their knives when it was a fish market.

There are around 40 shops in this little consumer paradise. These include a florist, sweet shop, tartan and kilt outlet, jewellery, barber, models, beauty therapy, clothes and fashion for adults and kiddies, newsagent, music and records, domestic spares and oriental food. There are also the Caley Thistle merchandise shop and the only bagpipe shop in the Highlands, so let's hear no complaints about lack of variety. The Victorian Market may not have the glitz and glamour of the Eastgate Centre but it's a cosier and much more interesting shopping area.

Index

(Proper names only. References to Inverness in general are not included. Page numbers in bold type indicate an entry devoted to the subject.)

Index (cont'd)

Index (cont'd)